| OC 03 '02 | DATE DUE | | |
|---|---|---|---|
| APR 0 3 '08 | | | |
| APR 2 1 '08 | | | |
| | | | |
| | | | |
| | | | |
| | | | |
| | | | |
| | | | |
| | | | |
| | | | |
| | | | |

LOOKING INTO THE PAST:
PEOPLE, PLACES, AND CUSTOMS

# Children of the World

by

Thomas Bracken

Chelsea House Publishers

**CHELSEA HOUSE PUBLISHERS**

*Editor-in-Chief* Stephen Reginald
*Managing Editor* James D. Gallagher
*Production Manager* Pamela Loos
*Art Director* Sara Davis
*Picture Editor* Judy Hasday
*Senior Production Editor* Lisa Chippendale
*Designers* Takeshi Takahashi, Keith Trego

First Printing

1 3 5 7 9 8 6 4 2

**Library of Congress Cataloging-in-Publication Data**

Bracken, Thomas
Children of the World / by Thomas Bracken.

 p. cm. —(Looking into the Past)
Includes bibliographical references and index.
Summary: Examines the different languages, national dress,
and social and cultural activities of children from various
countries of the world.

ISBN 0-7910-4685-0

1. Children—Cross-cultural studies—Juvenile literature.
[1. Manners and customs.] I. Title. II. Series.
GN482.B73   1997
305.23'071—dc21                              97-31058
                                                  CIP
                                                  AC

# CONTENTS

# CULTURE, CUSTOMS, AND RITUALS

The important moments of our lives—from birth through puberty, aging, and death—are made more meaningful by culture, customs, and rituals. But what is culture? The word *culture,* broadly defined, includes the way of life of an entire society. This encompasses customs, rituals, codes of manners, dress, languages, norms of behavior, and systems of beliefs. Individuals are both acted on by and react to a culture—and so generate new cultural forms and customs.

What is custom? Custom refers to accepted social practices that separate one cultural group from another. Every culture contains basic customs, often known as rites of transition or passage. These rites, or ceremonies, occur at different stages of life, from birth to death, and are sometimes religious in nature. In all cultures of the world today, a new baby is greeted and welcomed into its family through ceremony. Some ceremonies, such as the bar mitzvah, a religious initiation for teenage Jewish boys, mark the transition from childhood to adulthood. Marriage also is usually celebrated by a ritual of some sort. Death is another rite of transition. All known cultures contain beliefs about life after death, and all observe funeral rites and mourning customs.

What is a ritual? What is a rite? These terms are used interchangeably to describe a ceremony associated with a custom. The English ritual of shaking hands in greeting, for example, has become part of that culture. The washing of one's hands could be considered a ritual which helps a person achieve an accepted level of cleanliness—a requirement of the cultural beliefs that person holds.

The books in this series, *Looking into the Past: People,*

*Places, and Customs,* explore many of the most interesting rituals of different cultures through time. For example, did you know that in the year A.D. 1075 William the Conqueror ordered that a "Couvre feu" bell be rung at sunset in each town and city of England, as a signal to put out all fires? Because homes were made of wood and had thatched roofs, the bell served as a precaution against house fires. Today, this custom is no longer observed as it was 900 years ago, but the modern word *curfew* derives from its practice.

Another ritual that dates from centuries long past is the Japanese Samurai Festival. This colorful celebration commemorates the feats of the ancient samurai warriors who ruled the country hundreds of years ago. Japanese citizens dress in costumes, and direct descendants of warriors wear samurai swords during the festival. The making of these swords actually is a separate religious rite in itself.

Different cultures develop different customs. For example, people of different nations have developed various interesting ways to greet each other. In China 100 years ago, the ordinary salutation was a ceremonious, but not deep, bow, with the greeting "Kin t'ien ni hao ma?" (Are you well today?). During the same era, citizens of the Indian Ocean island nation Ceylon (now called Sri Lanka) greeted each other by placing their palms together with the fingers extended. When greeting a person of higher social rank, the hands were held in front of the forehead and the head was inclined.

Some symbols and rituals rooted in ancient beliefs are common to several cultures. For example, in China, Japan, and many of the countries of the East, a tortoise is a symbol of protection from black magic, while fish have represented fertility, new life, and prosperity since the beginnings of human civilization. Other ancient fertility symbols have been incorporated into religions we still practice today, and so these ancient beliefs remain a part of our civilization. A more recent belief, the legend of Santa Claus, is the story of a kind benefactor who brings gifts to the good children of the world. This story appears in the lore of nearly every nation. Each country developed its own variation on the legend and each celebrates Santa's arrival in a different way.

New rituals are being created all the time. On April 21, 1997, for example, the cremated remains of 24 people were launched into orbit around Earth on a Pegasus rocket. Included among the group whose ashes now head toward their "final frontier" are Gene Roddenberry, creator of the television series *Star Trek,* and Timothy Leary, a countercultural icon of the 1960s. Each person's remains were placed in a separate aluminum capsule engraved with the person's name and a commemorative phrase. The remains will orbit the Earth every 90 minutes for two to ten years. When the rocket does re-enter Earth's atmosphere, it will burn up with a great burst of light. This first-time ritual could become an accepted rite of passage, a custom in our culture that would supplant the current ceremonies marking the transition between life and death.

Curiosity about different customs, rites, and rituals dates back to the mercantile Greeks of classical times. Herodotus (484–425 B.C.), known as the "Father of History," described Egyptian culture. The Roman historian Tacitus (A.D. 55–117) similarly wrote a lengthy account about the customs of the "modern" European barbarians. From the Greeks to Marco Polo, from Columbus to the Pacific voyages of Captain James Cook, cultural differences have fascinated the literate world. The books in the *Looking into the Past* series collect the most interesting customs from many cultures of the past and explain their origins, meanings, and relationship to the present day.

In the future, space travel may very well provide the impetus for new cultures, customs, and rituals, which will in turn enthrall and interest the peoples of future millennia.

Fred L. Israel
*The City College of the City University of New York*

# CONTRIBUTORS

Senior Consulting Editor FRED L. ISRAEL is an award-winning historian. He received the Scribe's Award from the American Bar Association for his work on the Chelsea House series *The Justices of the United States Supreme Court*. A specialist in early American history, he was general editor for Chelsea's *1897 Sears Roebuck Catalog*. Dr. Israel has also worked in association with Dr. Arthur M. Schlesinger, jr. on many projects, including *The History of U.S. Presidential Elections* and *The History of U.S. Political Parties*. They are currently working together on the Chelsea House series *The World 100 Years Ago*, which looks at the traditions, customs, and cultures of many nations at the turn of the century.

THOMAS BRACKEN teaches American History at the City University of New York, and has taught at Mercy College. A former recipient of a grant from the Ford Foundation to conduct independent historical research, he created a CD-ROM to be used as a review guide in conjunction with college curriculums, and has published biographies of Theodore Roosevelt, William McKinley, and Abraham Lincoln. Mr. Bracken lives in New Jersey.

# OVERVIEW
# Children of the World

As we meet these children of the world dressed in their native costume, we immediately become aware how different they are from us. The languages they speak, the words they use, may seem strange, and even a bit funny. Instead of "please," they say "*s'il vous plaît*," "*per piacere*," or "*por favore*." Instead of "goodbye" they respond with "*au revoir*," "*a rivedercia*," or "*adios*." It makes us hesitate to say "hello!" But we do anyway. "*Bonjour*," "*buon giorno*," or "*buenos dias*," they reply.

The clothing pictured in this book also reveals something about the people who wore it many years ago. The native costumes of these children is a reflection of the national origins of the child wearing it.

The lessons these strange words and unfamiliar outfits teach is that although the citizens of the world's nations are different, they are also similar in many ways. Today, the differences that once divided us now seem to draw us closer together, as we learn how small this world is and how all the people in it are somehow connected.

For one brief moment, consider what is happening in the world at this moment. How many people are watching televisions or listening to radios that were made in countries far away from the ones they live in? What are you having for dinner tonight—Pizza? Tacos? A hamburger with French fries?

Through the things that we learn and the people that we meet, we are able to construct a shared body of attitudes and ideals for all people to believe in. The accumulation and sub-sequent use of this knowledge indicates an eagerness to become effective and responsible citizens of the world we all share. We do not, after all, seek to build walls around us, but, rather, to knock them down.

# ALASKA

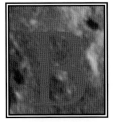

efore Alaska was admitted into the Union as the 49th state in 1959, young children there were educated in village traditions and native hunting-and-gathering skills. Now, however, their grade school education is nearly identical to that of all other American children. During the long, cold winter, many young Alaskans can be found playing hockey, skiing, snow-mobiling, and ice fishing. During the summer they love to play baseball and go camping with their parents.

The people of Alaska enjoy a year-round schedule of events that keeps the children of that state quite busy during all four seasons. Some of these special events are the Arctic Winter Games in March, the Eskimo-Indian Olympics festival in July, and the state's most famous event, the Iditarod dogsled race, which is usually held in late winter. Although Alaska is our northernmost state, the Fourth of July is still celebrated there with games of baseball and backyard barbecues, exactly as it is commemorated just about every-where else in the United States.

As winter temperatures sometimes drop to -40° F and some parts of the state can get more than 50 feet of snow in a single year, it is important for everyone—particularly chil-dren—to dress warmly. In the past, clothing was often made of animal skins, usually those of seal and caribou. Native Alaskans varied the decorative designs on their clothing to represent their tribes. In a land with such a cold climate, it is surprising to learn that sometimes the sun shines so brightly that children wore wooden hats to protect their eyes from its glare. Eskimo clothing usually was very func-tional: babies and very young children were often carried in the hoods of their parents' parkas.

# AUSTRALIA

he Aborigines are the native people of Australia, and their ancestors were the original inhabitants of that island continent. They have many distinct physical characteristics that set them apart from other people in Australia. These include hair that is usually curly or wavy, skin colors that range from tan to dark brown, and average-sized bodies with slender limbs. Today many Aborigines still obtain food by hunting and gathering assorted plants, and their early years are dedicated to learning these survival skills. Aborigine children do not live in any permanent form of housing, as their clans, or family groups, are constantly moving in search of food. Quite commonly, they live in huts made of grass and tree barks that are erected under large rock formations.

Young boys rarely join young girls in shared games and amusements; Aborigine girls are kept apart from the males in their communities, instead joining their mothers in special secret activities open to only women. While boys learn how to hunt large animals (sometimes with a boomerang), girls learn how to gather vegetables, fruits, and the eggs of birds, which they also learn how to cook.

Like virtually all other people of the world, however, Aborigine children love to express themselves through song and dance, and they have a uniquely rich oral tradition. Those who live in the colder parts of Australia usually wear cloaks that are made of kangaroo or possum fur. Aborigines in warmer regions wear little clothing. They do, however, enjoy wearing ornaments and decorative waistbands to liven up their simple outfits.

# BELGIUM

O ne of the favorite activities of Belgian children is participating in the traditional festivals and carnivals held every year in this country's cities and towns. The celebration that many love best of all is the one that takes place in the city of Bruges, in which participants reenact a medieval tournament that first took place over 600 years ago. Both boys and girls also love to ride their bicycles in Belgium, and soccer, fishing, and camping are very popular pastimes as well. One unusual hobby that many young Belgians enjoy is pigeon racing.

About 95 percent of the people in Belgium live in cities and towns, and a great number of them love to spend their vacations at the many resorts located on the coast of the North Sea. Belgians value their family ties very highly, and most families spend a lot of time together. The favorite room in a Belgian household is the kitchen. Here, family members cook some of their favorite foods, such as eel, rabbit, and French-fried potatoes with mayonnaise, and they also congregate to share their thoughts and ideas with one another.

The country is noted for the beautiful lace that it produces: many young girls learn how to make lace from their mothers at an early age. The pretty costume that you see here, with its deep lace collar and matching cap, might have been created at home by a skilled Belgian lacemaker.

# BRAZIL

There are two sides to Brazil: huge, bustling, modern cities such as São Paulo and Rio de Janeiro, and the dense Amazon rain forest. Although the Amazon region occupies more than half the territory of Brazil, it is populated by less than one percent of the country's people. The people who live in the rain forest still live in the same manner as their ancestors did in the days before America was discovered by Europeans over 500 years ago.

For these people, life in this hot, humid land is simple and unhurried. The men in each village hunt, fish, and gather wild nuts and fruits. Women busy themselves with farming, usually planting corn and yams. Families live together in houses with frames made of large bamboo poles and walls composed of nothing more than branches and leaves. The roofs are layers of palm leaves.

Because much of their land is covered with rivers and streams, canoeing is the most common method of transportation for these native Brazilians. Their canoes are made by hollowing out a type of tree that often grows taller than 50 feet. The traditional dress of the various native groups that inhabit the rain forest is very simple, usually consisting of nothing more than a few strips of cloth made from plant fibers. Sometimes girls will wear decorative patterns on their skirts. Both men and women cover themselves with large leaves for protection from the heavy rains that are common to the region.

Education for the children of these tribes consists of teaching them the skills that they will need for survival. For girls, these include making bread, and for boys, hunting and fishing.

# CHINA

amily life is particularly important in China. In fact, it is not uncommon for a young Chinese person to grow up with his or her grandparents in the same household. Both at home and at school, young children are almost always treated with great kindness and indulgence. It is not unusual for a Chinese child to begin nursery school as early as the age of two. But some Chinese children leave school after only six years. Children born in the city are more likely to continue in school and eventually attend college than children born in the countryside. As they grow up, children are encouraged to share their toys and to avoid fighting or arguing. Group activities, such as singing, organized games, and team sports, are encouraged as appropriate leisure activities. Solitary play is generally looked down upon.

As the Chinese alphabet has several thousand characters (as compared to 26 in the Roman alphabet used in the United States), it is particularly difficult for China's children to learn how to read and write. To help them prepare for this task, they are taught how to draw and paint at an early age in the hope that it will train their hands to draw the many complicated shapes and figures of their alphabet.

In China, both men and women traditionally wore a dark blue jacket. Working-class families dressed in plain clothes, with closed jackets and long tunics. The young Chinese boy pictured at left is wearing the clothing that he would wear even after he has reached adulthood.

# DENMARK

A drive through the picturesque Danish countryside of today is a most enjoyable experience. In addition to clear blue lakes and white sand beaches, it is not unusual to spot centuries-old castles and windmills in the country's carefully tended farmlands. The roofs of most rural houses in these areas are made of red or blue tile, and they are often home to stork's nests. But these birds are not unwelcome guests: Danish families believe that the stork brings good luck when it settles on top of houses.

The Danes keep their major cities scrupulously clean. Streets often appear to have been swept and mopped every single night. Danish people seldom stay inside when the weather is good, as they love outdoor sports, particularly rowing, swimming, and riding. In addition to these activities, Danish children look forward to visiting Tivoli Gardens, a world-famous amusement park in Copenhagen. Shooting galleries, circus acts, fireworks displays and rides are just some of its attractions, along with delicious foods like *smorrebrod*, a favorite kind of open-faced sandwich.

As Danish women are excellent embroiderers, they often decorate their clothing with gaily-colored stitchery. The traditional Danish costume shown here is often worn at the many folk festivals celebrated annually throughout the country.

# EGYPT

early half of all young Egyptians live in the country, and for them life is a continuous cycle of farm chores. They bring water into the fields to help irrigate the crops, and they also tend livestock. These children belong to a class called *fellahin*. They usually live in very small huts made of mud bricks and topped with straw roofs. Most of these huts have no more than three rooms, but they do come equipped with a courtyard where the family can keep its animals. Egyptian children love goat's milk, sheep's milk—even buffalo's milk!

Soccer is the country's most popular sport, and young fans like to root for their favorite teams when they are not participating themselves. But the main recreational outlet for children of all ages in Egypt is a trip to the local bazaar, which is an outdoor market filled with shops and restaurants. They will often accompany their parents there to catch up on the latest news with friends and neighbors. The small villages that *fellahin* children live in offer ample opportunities to join with their neighbors in celebrating special occasions, such as marriages and births.

Most Egyptian children whose parents are not very rich—regardless of where they live—wear traditional clothing. Boys wear full, shirtlike garments called *galabiyahs*, while girls wear long, brightly-colored gowns. Silver anklets are a favorite accessory of Egyptian children.

# ENGLAND

One of the favorite holidays of English children is Guy Fawkes Day, which is celebrated on November 5. On that day, children make stuffed dummies, which they call "guys," and playfully try to collect money by asking everyone they meet if they can spare "a penny for the guy." At nightfall, there are great fireworks displays throughout the entire country and the dummies are burned in huge bonfires. For day-to-day entertainment, English children love to see movies at the cinema. Cricket, soccer, and rugby are the most popular sports among boys, but both boys and girls enjoy golf, tennis, and riding. Children also love to visit England's popular seacoast resorts and join their parents in swimming and games on the beach during vacations.

The British love a full breakfast, so English children often start their day with a meal consisting of bacon and eggs, smoked herring, and cold meats served with porridge and toast. Families also look forward to a Sunday dinner of roast beef, potatoes, and turnips.

Although most English people dress just like Americans, some people still envision the "typical Englishman," who wears a dark coat and border hat while carrying an umbrella under his arm. The young boy shown here attends one of England's private schools, at which both boys and girls are required to wear uniforms.

# FRANCE

rench children eagerly look forward to Christmas Day, called Noël, when their families hold huge gatherings at which they receive presents. Other favorite holidays include Easter, or Paques, when children receive chocolate chickens and colored candy eggs, and Shrove Tuesday, which is celebrated in many provinces by a merry and colorful festival called Carnival.

One of the many things that France is noted for is its good food, and children enjoy a wide variety of tasty dishes. Among their favorites are *bouillabaisse*, a seafood stew; *crepes*, which are thinly rolled pancakes; and *quiche*, or custard baked in a pastry shell.

The French do more than just eat, however. Children of all ages eagerly anticipate the Tour de France, the most popular sporting event in the country. This is a grueling bicycle race that runs every summer, lasts for nearly a month, and passes through almost the entire country. French children like to participate in soccer, ice skating, and boules, a game similar to bowling. Camping is a popular vacation activity that millions of French families enjoy every year.

Paris, the largest city in France, is the fashion capital of the world; accordingly, French fashion designers have influenced international style for years. Traditional French peasant dress is usually flamboyant and bright, with each province of the country adding some distinguishing feature to its local clothing. In the past, different professions also had specific clothing styles. The young boy you see here is wearing a blouse and beret typical of a French artist.

# GREECE

reek children love to take evening walks with their parents, either to window-shop or just to catch up on the latest news with their neighbors. In the cities, boys often accompany their fathers to the local coffee house to play backgammon; in the country, girls frequently join their mothers for daily strolls to the local churchyard or fountain. The children of Greece are encouraged to be curious, freedom-loving, and quick-witted—just as their ancestors were.

In traditional Greek restaurants, popular dishes include stuffed grape leaves, a wide variety of lamb dishes, and a soft white cheese made from goat's milk called *feta*.

Religious festivals play an important role in the lives of most Greek people, and nearly every town or village has its own patron saint. On the feast of their town's patron saint, Greek children join their parents in singing and dancing late into the night. Children in Greece do not exchange presents on Christmas Day, but rather on St. Basil's Day, which falls on January 1. On this special occasion, they often don the traditional dress of Greek peasants: boys will wear long woolen tights and pleated kilts, and girls will wear long, bright skirts with white blouses. These blouses are usually adorned with silver buttons and embroidered with red and yellow thread. Favorite fashions for girls include scarves in pale pastel colors and aprons worn with heavy leather belts.

# HOLLAND

t times, life in the Netherlands, also known as Holland, seems to be one festival after another for its young residents. Presents are exchanged on St. Nicholas's Eve instead of Christmas Day. Children throughout Holland believe that St. Nicholas rewards them for a year of good behavior by leaving presents at their homes. Another special day for Dutch children is Palm Sunday, when young people throughout the country sing joyous Easter songs in merry, lantern-lit parades. These parades stop in the center of each town for extended sessions of music and dance, in which children are encouraged to participate. One week later, on Easter Sunday, they play a series of games, all of which involve colored eggs. Still another favorite day is Queen's Day, April 30, when each town celebrates with its own *kermis*, a combination of carnival rides and other forms of entertainment.

When helping their parents raise the tulips and other bulb flowers for which Holland is famous, boys and girls alike wear outfits consisting of full skirts and straight, snug bodices. But boys only wear this costume until they are about seven years old, at which time they adopt the dress of grown men. It is common for Dutch children to wear clothing adorned with flower patterns. Many children living in fishing villages or on farms stilll wear the famous wooden shoes of Holland, called *klompen*. This traditional footwear protects their feet from the wet earth better than other shoes can. Children do not wear these noisy shoes indoors, however.

# INDIA

hildren in India who grow up in large households in the country have plenty of playmates, and the elders that care for them often pamper them with loving attention. But life is not carefree for the young people of India: by the time a boy reaches his eighth birthday, he may already be helping his father in the fields or with the family's livestock. Girls of the same age will probably be helping their mothers carry well water into their homes. Girls may also learn the delicate science of Indian spice mixing at a very early age. There are few amusements available for the poor peasants of India to enjoy other than weddings, religious festivals, and other celebrations. Wrestling matches and cockfights are the only regular forms of entertainment for many people in the country.

Most children in India live in houses made of mud and bamboo, which are placed very closely together in densely populated villages. During their school years many boys and girls are formally trained to play the *sitar*, a guitar-like instrument that one plays while sitting on the floor.

Although most city dwellers in India are adopting a taste for Western attire, those who live in the countryside still wear traditional clothing. Women still wear their lovely *saris*, long, flowing garments that wrap around the hip and drape over the shoulder or head. Saris are bordered in gold and silver thread when women can afford to do so. Many girls in India, particularly Hindus, decorate their foreheads with a dot of red powder or a tiny disc which is called a *kumkum*.

# IRELAND

lmost half the children of Ireland live in its beautiful green countryside, where farming is a major occupation. They enjoy close family ties, and some learn at an early age to develop their skills at storytelling, a gift for which the Irish are famous. Irish children study two languages in school: English and Gaelic, an ancient Celtic language. Young Irish boys love to ride and race horses. Other favorite sports include soccer, Gaelic football (which resembles soccer), and hurling (which resembles field hockey). Sports that both boys and girls enjoy include fishing, swimming, and tennis. Young girls learn from their mothers how to prepare delicacies like Irish stew, corned beef and cabbage, and scone.

The typical Irish child lives in a house made of brick or concrete with anywhere from four to seven rooms. Many Irish boys in the western town of Connemara observe a quaint Irish custom of wearing petticoats with the hope of confusing an evil fairy who runs off with boys, but not girls. Many young girls love to wear shawls and Kerry cloaks to add color and style to their outfits.

Next to Christmas, a young Irish person's favorite day of the year is probably St. Patrick's Day. Celebrated on March 17, St. Patrick's Day is the national holiday of Ireland. Many children march in festive parades on that day before joining their families in celebrations filled with music and dance.

# ITALY

Italian children enjoy a wide variety of sports, with soccer the most popular by far. Every major city in Italy has its own professional team, and on weekends nearly every park is filled with children playing the game and dreaming that one day they will be good enough to compete for the World Cup. Basketball is another favorite sport of Italian children. Others include fishing, bicycling, and roller skating.

Family life is very important to the Italians, and eating is a favorite family activity. Italian children relish foods such as pasta and *risotto*, a rice dish made with seafood, meat, or vegetables. They will often take these foods on picnics or enjoy them as part of the long, relaxed weekend meals which are themselves a form of recreation for the people of Italy. Another favorite recreational activity is the *passeggiata*, or family stroll, as well as trips to the mountains or seaside.

Most Italian children living in the north dwell in cities, while most in the south reside in small towns or villages. Rome and Milan, the two largest cities of the country, are centers of world fashion.

In addition to Christmas, Easter is eagerly awaited by the young people of Italy. On that day they dress in their fanciest clothes and join in local parades and processions. Italians traditionally wore colorful costumes accompanied by a lot of jewelry. The girl in this illustration, with a kerchief on her head to protect her from the sun, is probably from southern Italy.

# JAPAN

ost Japanese children live in cities, as theirs is one of the most densely populated countries in the entire world. Many young boys develop an early interest in a unique form of wrestling called *Sumo*, in addition to the martial arts of *akido*, *judo*, and *karate*.

A favorite Japanese holiday is the New Year's Day Festival, which begins on January 1. At home, families exchange gifts, play traditional Japanese games, and enjoy rich, sumptuous meals, after which they don their fanciest clothes to visit friends and relatives. Parades, dances, and sporting events are held throughout the country, and these fesitivities often last for two full weeks. May 5 is also eagerly awaited, as it is a national celebration set apart especially for children.

In a Japanese family, the oldest son is expected to carry on his father's profession, and Japanese children grow up with strong family ties and deep respect for parental authority. When they get older, some enter into marriages arranged by their parents, but this is becoming increasingly rare.

Although most Japanese wear Western-style clothing similar to that worn in the United States, they have always placed great emphasis on traditional costume for special occasions. At such times, children often wear kimonos and obis, which girls tie with a butterfly bow.

# JORDAN

ordan is situated in the Middle East, birthplace of three of the world's most prevalent religions: Judaism, Christianity, and Islam. Most of the people of Jordan are Muslims, or followers of Islam, and many Jordanian children speak both English and Arabic. Most children in Jordan live in cities or towns, in houses made of stone and mud. When not at school—which they are required to attend through the ninth grade—rural children may help their parents raise chickens and goats and tend crops. In school, young Jordanians learn the beautiful Arabic handwriting known as calligraphy; at home, many girls learn to do the elaborate cross-stitched embroidery that Jordan is famous for.

One unusual sport that children in Jordan love to watch is camel racing, but they actively participate in soccer and basketball. Another favorite pastime is joining friends and family for picnics in the country. At family gatherings they love to dance the *debke*, a native folk dance. While enjoying these family gatherings, many boys and girls feast on *mansef*, a traditional meal of lamb cooked in yogurt and served over rice.

While many Jordanians wear Western-style clothes, some who live in the country still wear their traditional long, flowing robes, and men may cover their heads with a garment called a *kaffiyeh*. Girls wear dresses made of dark linen with belts made of multicolored cashmere. Jackets edged with colorful embroidery are also popular.

# MEXICO

exican children grow up eager to learn how to perform the famous hat dance of their country, which is properly called the *jarabe tapitio*. They also look forward to learning the traditional folk songs of Mexico, called *corridos*, which tell the stories of brave Mexican heroes from the past in music. As they learn the steps to the hat dance, they tap their heels and toes and hop nimbly across the floor, sometimes to the music of the marimba, an instrument similar to the xylophone. Music and dance are elements of a fiesta, which Mexican children love to attend.

While they may not spend much time on fun and games, the children of Mexico get a deep feeling of satisfaction from helping their parents with household or farm chores. On Sundays, Mexican families may relax together on picnics. Some also watch their favorite sports: soccer, baseball, and bullfighting.

Many Mexican children like to dress in the traditional style of their country's various native groups as well as in modern styles. Some items of dress popularly associated with Mexico are the *sombrero*, a wide-brimmed hat made of felt or straw which is used as a protection from the sun, the *pancho*, a blanket that has an opening in the center for the head, and the *serape*, which serves as a blanket at night and is worn over one shoulder during the day.

# NORWAY

orway is known as the Land of the Midnight Sun, and its people have a reputation for strong will, industry, and thrift. Norwegians are also a very hardy people who generally enjoy a long life span. The children of Norway often grow up in sturdy homes situated in small towns or villages. The people of this northern country employ an unusual method of keeping warm during the long, snowy winters: they pack snow around their houses as tightly as possible. This traps the heat inside, providing the house's occupants with extra warmth.

Norwegian children love to ski and skate, and they are often taught to do both soon after they learn to walk. During the short Norwegian summers, they enjoy mountain climbing. Two important days of a Norwegian child's year are Midsummer's Eve (June 23), and Christmas Eve (December 24). Children join in Midsummer's Eve parades carrying small fir trees. Singing and dancing complete the festivities. On Christmas Eve, hopeful children leave a dish of pudding out for the Christmas elf. After he eats it, the story goes, he will reward the good children of Norway with presents.

Many small towns in Norway hold annual festivals to preserve the folk dances and costumes of the past. At these celebrations, girls can show off their traditional skirts of scarlet wool, along with their fashionable buckled leather shoes.

# POLAND

ew Europeans are more deeply aware of their past than the Poles, and this awareness is reflected in their preservation of traditional Polish music, dance, and costume. The overwhelming majority of Poles are Catholics. Because of this, Christmas and Easter are the most eagerly anticipated days of the year among Polish children. One of the biggest events in the life of a Catholic child in Poland is his or her first Holy Communion, which usually occurs between the ages of 6 and 10. The social life of most Poles centers around church and family gatherings. On special occasions, three generations of a Polish family might gather for a lively day of dancing, singing, and eating.

In Poland, education is mandatory for both boys and girls from the ages of seven to fifteen. Camping and hiking rank high among their favorite hobbies. Many Polish boys grow up to be skilled craftsmen in such trades as pottery and woodcarving. Girls often learn how to make beautiful lace from their mothers. A Polish girl may dream of her wedding day. On this occasion, bridal attendants dress in traditional Polish folk costumes. Traditional dress for Polish children usually incorporates bright colors worn in unexpected combinations, such as cherry red and brown. Girls wear their hair in long plaits, which are often tied with large bows and fancy ribbons.

# RUSSIA

E ducation is very important in the lives of young Russians. All students must pass annual exams to advance to their next level at school, and they must remain in school until age 17. The typical Russian child lives in a small apartment in a city. In these apartments, children join their parents in a midday meal—the biggest repast of the day in Russia. Very often this meal consists of *blinis* (thin pancakes served with sour cream) or *piroshki* (fried dumplings filled with cabbage and meat).

Virtually all Russian boys and girls love playing sports, particularly team sports. Their favorites include gymnastics, ice skating, and skiing. Children throughout the country can join special clubs devoted to playing their favorite sports. Chess is another popular game among Russian children. Some also pursue a unique hobby—picking mushrooms—when they visit the countryside.

Most people in Russia wear plain, simple clothes, and those Russian shoppers who want to buy the Western fashions that are rapidly becoming popular sometimes have difficulty finding them. On special occasions, such as weddings and holidays, rural Russians still wear their traditional dress, which for women consists of embroidered skirts and blouses. Woven belts and short bodices with sleeves made of hand-printed linen are popular among girls.

# SCOTLAND

oys and girls in Scotland love to dance the highland fling, the Scottish reel, and the sword dance, often competing in dance contests held all over the country. Other events at these competitions include footraces and association football (soccer). Many Scottish children learn to play golf at a very young age, probably because this internationally popular game originated here.

Another favorite pastime of Scottish children is reading. The authors of *Ivanhoe*, *Treasure Island*, and *Peter Pan* were all born in Scotland, so this small country has a rich literary tradition.

Children living in the rugged countryside help their parents with sheep shearing, an activity very important to the wool industry that thrives in the Highlands. Many children learn to perform this delicate task armed only with a pair of hand clippers.

For many people, Scotland brings to mind the plaintive sound of bagpipes, which are played on both joyous and somber occasions, and the bright plaids of Scottsmen's kilts. These skirt-like garments are usually made of wool. Each of the ancient Scottish clans, has its own distinctive plaid pattern, or tartan, which no one else is allowed to wear.

# SPAIN

occer is the most popular sport among children throughout Spain, but boys growing up in the city may also dream of the day when they become toreadors and engage in Spain's most famous spectator sport, bullfighting. The Feast of St. Fermin is held in the city of Pamplona every July to celebrate Spain's bullfighting tradition. Throughout the city, masses of people clad in native costume march through the streets to the strains of traditional Spanish music. Christmas and Spanish Labor Day, a national holiday that falls on July 18, are also significant dates.

Choral singing is a popular pastime among the Spanish. Every year, each of the country's 15 regions holds its own folk festival to showcase local music and dancing. Spanish children look forward to these festivals, where they might fill themselves with *cocido*, a dish that resembles stew.

An interesting feature of the way Spanish children dress is that the color of their clothing indicates their parents' economic status: the poorer people living in the countryside generally sport brightly colored clothes, while the wealthier people who dwell in the cities usually wear darker clothes. A particularly popular fashion among well-to-do Spanish girls is a long black dress. The girl in this picture is also wearing a *mantilla*, a veil made of black or white lace. It is anchored to the back of her head by a large comb. Mantillas, like black dresses, are worn regularly only by the higher classes.

# SWEDEN

**S**wedish children look forward to celebrating Christmas, Midsummer's Eve, and the feast of St. Lucia (December 13), who is revered by the Swedes as "the queen of lights." Swedish children also engage in a wide variety of sports. Skiing, skating, ice hockey and bandy, an ice game played with a ball, are some of their favorites. They are also fond of sailing and hiking. A mealtime treat for young Swedes is the smorgasbord, an assortment of snacks that often contains such seafood delicacies as herring, eel, and salmon.

In some parts of the country, such as Gotland, and Varmland, centuries-old customs are cherished, with both children and adults donning traditional peasant costumes at annual folk festivals. At these festivals, the townspeople gather to eat, dance, sing, and play games.

Traditional children's shoes are dyed in unusual colors and decorated with eye-catching designs. The buttons on their embroidered white blouses are often quite fancy, frequently made of silver and glass. The girl in the illustration wears a traditional bonnet, but does not tie it about her neck. She will continue to wear it this way until she is married to signal that she has yet to meet her husband.

# SWITZERLAND

iking in the lofty Alps is one of the favorite pastimes of Swiss children. But Switzerland is known for many things other than its beautiful mountains. The country is also associated with fine watches, an excellent banking system, and delicious chocolates. Switzerland is also known for remaining neutral in armed conflicts. The country has not engaged in any war since the early 1500s—a fact of which its citizens are very proud.

Most Swiss children like outdoor sports like bicycling, skiing, bobsledding, and camping. Another favorite game is *Hornussen*. This sport is somewhat like baseball, except that the batter hits a wooden disc with a wooden club that can measure up to eight feet long! Young Swiss men devote much of their time to target shooting, and local marksmanship contests are held frequently. Almost every Swiss town or village has its own singing group that practices weekly for local festivals and national vocal competitions. Band music is also very popular, as is folk dancing, which is often done in traditional costume.

The pretty Swiss girl shown here is wearing a chemisette with short puffed sleeves finished with ribbons at the elbows. The "halo" that fringes her bonnet is probably made of horsehair lace and stiffened with wire to keep it in place.

# UNITED STATES

I t is hard to describe a "typical" child in the United States, for the country is both vast and varied. Some children live on isolated farms; others live in cities teeming with millions of inhabitants. Some have parents who were born in distant countries and speak languages other than English; others are able to trace their family tree in America back more than 300 years.

But regardless of all the ways in which they may differ, the children of the United States share many common interests. Most grow up loving their country and their parents, and many study very hard in school. Boys and girls love to play sports, and they also enjoy watching the games between their favorite professional teams. Basketball, football, and baseball are favorite team sports, and tennis, running, and swimming are popular individual endeavors. Most children in the United States love to go to the movies, and many more enjoy such diverse hobbies as photography, card collecting, and listening to music. On the Fourth of July, they celebrate their country's birthday by eating hamburgers and hot dogs at family picnics and watching fireworks displays.

Pastimes of contemporary American children include playing with their computers or "hanging out" with their friends at the mall. They now prefer to dress as casually as possible, favoring blue jeans, T-shirts, and sneakers. Today's fashions contrast sharply with the old-fashioned dress of the young girl in this picture.

# CHILDREN IN NATIVE DRESS TIMELINE

**1523–1027 B.C.** The first documented civilization in China is the Shang dynasty. During this period, the Chinese built cities, developed bronze tools, weapons, and ornaments, and created a system of writing.

**A.D. 1291** The beginning of the Swiss Confederation can be traced back to this year with the signing of the Perpetual Covenant, a mutual defense treaty of the Swiss cantons. Switzerland adopted its constitution in 1848.

**1479** Modern Spain emerges with the union of Aragon and Castile. Previously, the country was a loose confederation of Christian kingdoms that had seized control of the country from the Moors.

**1707** The Kingdom of Great Britain is officially established with passage of the Act of Union, which joined England with Wales and the Kingdom of Scotland.

**1757** The British East India Company gains control of India. The next year, Great Britain took formal possession of the country, ruling it until India became independent in 1947.

**1770** Captain James Cook claims Australia for Great Britain. The island continent was established as a penal colony in 1788.

**1772** The area of Poland is partitioned by Austria, Prussia, and Russia. Poland declared itself an independent nation in 1918.

**1776** The Declaration of Independence marks the beginnings of the United States of America. The American Constitution was adopted in 1787.

**1792** As a result of the French Revolution of 1789 the First Republic of France is established in this year.

**1798** Egypt is captured by Napoleon Bonaparte of France. The period of French rule was brief, however, and in 1801 the country came under British rule. Egypt was awarded independence in 1922, and became a republic in 1953.

**1801** Ireland becomes part of the Kingdom of Great Britain. The Irish Free State was established in 1921, and in 1949 Ireland declared itself a republic.

**1830** Belgium officially becomes independent.

**1844** Greece, formerly part of the Ottoman Empire, becomes a constitutional monarchy.

**1849** Denmark adopts its first constitution. Previously, the country had been united with Norway and Sweden.

**1861** The Kingdom of Italy is formed. Previously, the loose confederation of Italian states was part of the Holy Roman Empire.

**1867** Alaska is purchased from Russia by the United States. It was established as a territory in 1912, and on January 3, 1959, admitted into the U.S. as the 49th state.

**1917** The Bolsheviks revolt against Czarist rule in Russia. In 1922, the communist Union of Soviet Socialist Republics (U.S.S.R.) was established. The U.S.S.R. was dissolved in 1991, when Russia and the Soviet republics declared themselves independent.

**1948** Palestine, one of the world's most important historical regions, is divided between Jordan, Egypt, and Israel.

**1949** Chinese communists proclaim the People's Republic of China with Mao Tse-Tung as chairman.

# INDEX ❦

# Further Reading

Ewing, Elizabeth. *History of Children's Costume*. New York: Scribner, 1977.

Joy, Charles. *Young People of Central Europe*. New York: Duell, Sloan, and Pearce, 1966.

_____. *Young People of Western Europe: Their stories in Their Own Words*. New York: Meredith Press, 1967.

Mead, Margaret. *Childhood in Contemporary Culture*. Chicago: University of Chicago Press, 1969.

Nieri, Lorraine. *Dear American Friends: Letters from School Children Around the World*. New York: Vanguard Press, 1960.

Opie, Iona. *The People in the Playground*. New York: University Press, 1993.

Sichel, Marion. *History of Children's Costume*. New York: Chelsea House Publishers, 1977.

Wheatley, Nadia. *My Place*. New York: Kane/Miller Book Publishers, 1992.